DR. DAMARY BONILLA-RODRIGUEZ

MODERN MARIANISMO
ITS RELEVANCE AND THE CONNECTION TO IMPOSTOR SYNDROME AND PERFECTIONISM

MODERN MARIANISMO
ITS RELEVANCE AND THE CONNECTION TO IMPOSTOR SYNDROME AND PERFECTIONISM

©Copyright 2024, Damary Bonilla-Rodriguez
All rights reserved.

No portion of this book may be reproduced by mechanical, photographic, or electronic process; nor may it be stored in a retrieval system, transmitted in any form, or otherwise be copied for public use or private use without written permission of the copyright owner.

It is sold with the understanding that the publisher and the individual author are not engaged in the rendering of psychological, legal, accounting, or other professional advice. The content and views in this book are the sole expression and opinion of the author and not necessarily the views of Fig Factor Media, LLC.

For More Information:
Fig Factor Media | figfactormedia.com
Cover Design by Marco Alvarez and Layout by LDG Manuel Serna Rosales

Printed in the United States of America

ISBN: 978-1-952779-31-2
Library of Congress Control Number: 2024901234

DEDICATION

I dedicate this book to the amazing women who've poured into me so that I could become who I am today.

A special dedication to my mother, Edith Damary, who died at age 27 but left a deep imprint in my heart of her love, strength and rebellious nature. She was eight in this photo and that's how old I was when she passed away. My eight-year-old self remembers how she struggled to navigate her passions and desires against the boundaries set for her by others. My mom's last role was a school bus driver. I was so proud and still today, I think the world of female bus drivers. She wasn't able to fully break free from expectations but her premature departure influenced my freedom from generational cycles of self-doubt and patterns of oppression. RIP my badass mommy. I will always love you.

"Each time a woman stands up for herself, she stands up for all women."
—Maya Angelou

TABLE OF CONTENTS

Acknowledgments 5
Foreword 6
Introduction 8

Calling out the Triumvirate 11
Exploring Machismo and Marianismo 17
Why Talk about Marianismo? 25
Effects of The Impostor Syndrome 33
Perfection Doesn't Exist 37
Surviving Interconnected Ideologies 41
Redefining Gender Expectations 45
Developing Your Identity 49
Understanding Modern Marianismo 55
Overcoming the Triumvirate 61
    Work Through Vulnerability 63
    Identify with Transformational Leadership 65
    Accept Partnership 67
    Tap Your Spiritual Beliefs 69
    Give Yourself Grace 73
The Marianismo Anthem 77
About the Author 80

ACKNOWLEDGMENTS

The writing journey is empowering but exhausting and brings one to a place of vulnerability that pours onto the pages that you hope will resonate for every reader. In my case, I was living and navigating through the topics I was writing about so I experienced challenges along the way that delayed completion. However, I am blessed to have people in my life that uplift and encourage me when I'm empty from juggling my many roles.

My accomplishments have always come to fruition because of my loved ones and supporters; the reality is that no one can do everything alone. Hence, why I must acknowledge those who've been along this journey with me and because this finished product wouldn't have come forth without each of you.

First, to God be the glory for being the head of our home and sustaining us. I also honor my husband, who is the priest of our home, my partner in life, and my number one fan. Hunny, you've pushed me when I didn't think I had anything left and you've carried me when I threw my hands up. Rob, I love you and am grateful that you believe in me unconditionally and share me with those who need me to advocate for them.

The public leadership path is a tough one but my boys motivate me to fight for a better society, where they'll have opportunities to succeed. Joshua and Caleb, you're my reasons for working so hard and forging ahead through adversity. Our talks help me to understand current issues; your love and encouraging words give me strength on tough days. Mommy loves you dearly.

Family has always played an important role in my life, from my aunts and uncles filling in on parental aspects that were missing due to loss from a young age to my nieces, nephews and godchildren for building my drive for social justice because of the serious situations they live with that have required my advocacy to ensure their access to my sisters who I've always strived to be a role model and mother figure for since we lost our mom as kids. I'm better because of their genuine love and ongoing support. All of you hold a special place in my heart.

Friends and colleagues, thank you for keeping me focused through kind gestures and heart-to-heart talks, especially my BFF. To the prayer warriors, thank you for covering me. For institutions that have hired me since I launched Dr. Damary Bonilla-Rodriguez and Associates LLC, thank you for validating the need for this book. I'm grateful that you're all a part of my life.

Bringing acknowledgments to full circle, I must thank my amazing publisher, Jackie. You've wanted me to write this book since we met over a decade ago and helped me tell my story through *Today's Inspired Latina*. I'm humbled and grateful for your patience and thought partnership over the past fifteen months, along with a strong commitment from the brilliant Fig Factor Media team.

Last but not least, I honor the memory of my mom, grandparents and loved ones who are no longer physically present. They're with me in spirit and their influence inspires me to keep going.

"I can do all things through Christ who strengthens me." —**Philippians 4:13**

FOREWORD

I'll never forget meeting Dr. Damary Bonilla-Rodriguez. She was a teen participant in a leadership program sponsored by Girls Incorporated, which inspires girls to be "strong, smart, and bold." I was immediately drawn to one of the teens who was incredibly confident, poised, and very talkative. Of course, it was Damary. At the time, I was the chair of the board of directors, the first Latina to serve in that role. As I heard more about this extraordinary teenager's life through this program, our bond grew.

Despite growing up in challenging circumstances, Damary had dreams and aspirations that she wanted to pursue. She envisioned a better life for herself and her family. Even though Damary looked to me as a mentor, I learned just as much from her.

Like many of you and Dr. Damary, I have had the burden and honor of being the "one" and "only" in roles that had never before been held by a Latina. As one of the first Latinas to earn partnership at a major law firm, I saw firsthand how challenging it can be to feel alone. Even as I joined several prestigious boards, I continued to feel acutely aware of being the only person in the room who looked like me. My experience throughout my professional life inspired me to pay it forward through dismantling the barriers so many of us face.

Throughout the past thirty years, I have watched Dr. Damary overcome challenges on personal and professional levels. I watched as she graduated high school, then pursued and earned several degrees. She rose from poverty to the ranks of a small number of Latinas in the United States with a doctorate. Dr. Damary is a shining example of the power of educational access, perseverance, and determination to push against social standards, which can hinder Latinas and women from achieving the greatness within them.

In this book, Dr. Damary describes the factors relating to gender expectations and cultural nuances to those factors that might be holding you back. Her goal is to empower you to take control of your life and leadership journey and decide what values, decisions, and responsibilities to consider as you forge your path and define success for yourself.

Dr. Damary describes how our experiences, no matter our age or educational background, impact us in ways that are hard to comprehend. She shows how a CEO or a stay-at-home mom can both be weighed down by trying to be perfect. The fear of being an impostor exists within all of us.

Expounding on a term she coined in her doctoral research, Dr. Damary names cultural aspects many women face and encourages us to move from Marianismo to Modern Marianismo. Her research shows how reconciling our cultural divides free us to stop feeling crippling pressure. Furthermore, she outlines how Marianismo, Perfectionism and the Impostor Syndrome are interconnected. She posits that if you experience one, you will likely experience them all.

The good news is that there is hope for each of us to work through any situation before us. Dr. Damary poses questions to help you think through your challenges, strategies to get you moving in the right direction, and resources to support your journey to your greatest self. This book will be foundational for your leadership breakthrough and an indispensable guide to move you forward.

Regina Montoya, Attorney, Civic Volunteer and Philanthropist

INTRODUCTION

Society has always operated through norms; managing expectations for acceptable behaviors that will ensure functionality. The interesting aspect here is that such norms have emerged from a patriarchal structure, which lends itself to male-dominated gender norms. We see this show up through expressions such as: "men don't cry," "gay men aren't manly enough," "sports are for men," etc. Traditional expectations are not favorable to driving an inclusive and respectable society, where women, people of color, and other marginalized individuals have equal chances to secure visible, high-level leadership roles.

In an era of heightened social justice advocacy and the fight for equity, one would hope these issues were resolved. But when people are categorized as a method to track who is moving where or who is doing what, power struggles are guaranteed. Affix cultural nuances to the equation and you have a formula for inequity.

Systems, policies, and practices have been historically weaponized by those in authority to prevent change, especially relating to people from marginalized communities. Power and leadership dynamics, which hamper equitable experiences and opportunities, ought to be dismantled and re-created. I say this not just for the sake of change but to allow the authentic exchange of diverse experiences and beliefs to guide a culture of equity where women, the LGBTQIA+ community, and people of color, are no longer treated as unequal members of society.

As an advocate for more diverse, equitable, and inclusive (DEI) spaces throughout society, I'm sensitive to the comments that the quest for DEI is too much or pointing out a specific group as wanting too many rights. Pushback in this form stems from fear and trust issues. What does this mean in the fight for social justice?

Some are fearful about how society will change, if we allow freedom of expression and lifestyles that don't align with their religious beliefs. Others who have been in power are worried to lose it and, therefore, lose control. This is especially worrisome for some who aren't comfortable with a society where everyone feels they belong and can be authentic; they interpret these efforts as threats to their positions of influence by people who are not from the same demographic groups as they are.

Factor in the *isms* to get a clear picture of what is causing the mind of someone who is racist, sexist, homophobic, and just can't process a world in which 'those people' hold the highest seat anywhere. Negativity shows up in comments, character attacks, and unfair legislation, and there are no limits to the extent to which people will encroach on people for how they identify.

Who granted anyone permission to write the code of conduct for others, especially to make them oppressive towards particular groups? The rules of engagement are flawed because they give precedence to one gender, contributing to unfair treatment of the other. Good news though, men can serve as allies to women in the quest for equity and relief from autocratic conduct perpetuated by a patriarchal society.

Males, who hold decision-making positions, can push for fair policies and ensure equal pay for women. Advocacy, at all levels, will finally tip the scale to even out fairness towards women and all people. Truthfully, everyone could do a better job of treating others with respect, dignity, and equality without deeming specific identifiers as an indicator or whether someone deserves good or bad treatment.

CALLING OUT **THE TRIUMVIRATE**

We cannot allow antiquated dynamics and patriarchal inclination to slow us down from leading change and sharing our brilliance with the world. The societal dynamic shift that I envision is a prime juncture for women to take their place at the table, especially women of color. Our lived experiences enable us to redefine challenges into successes and keep an open-minded approach to leadership. This charge is what we're coining as *The Marianismo Anthem*.

One particular aspect we bring to any role is an understanding of how cultural nuances impact the needs and desires of people who look, talk, eat, dance, dress, and love differently from the expectations of mainstream American society. Rewriting the diversity narrative is imperative to achieving true equity and dismantling pervasive despotism, which feeds the surmising of our supposed inadequacy and leading to the Triumvirate we're unmasking here. It is an interconnectedness between Marianismo, the Impostor Syndrome, and Perfectionism.

In a venture to identify the feelings, thoughts, and stressors that immerse us into a whirlwind perilous to our success, we will refer to Triumvirate differently than it has been historically defined. I'm using the term to elucidate what many experience but cannot articulate about their struggle to prevail over the three ideologies (Marianismo, the Impostor Syndrome and Perfectionism). You see, there is power in words. Sometimes words are weaponized to manipulate, confuse, and hurt people. However, my aim is to inspire, empower, and educate people through words. Therefore, I'm reframing a unique term meant to capture the power hoarding arrangement of three men in several historical instances to explain the depth of power that these three ideologies have held over many of us.

The First Triumvirate dates back to 60 BC when Marcus Lucinius Crassus, Gaius Julius Caesar I and Gnaius Pompeius Magnus (Pompey) made a pact for shared ruling to control all of Rome and advance their respective agendas. Individual desires eventually led to the demise of their agreement. The Second Triumvirate also took place in Rome in 43 BC with consent of the Senate for Gaius Julius Caesar Octavianus (Octavian), Marcus Aemilius Lepidus, and Marcus Antonius (Mark Antony). They established a political partnership to avenge Caesar's death and stabilize Rome. However, disputes and distrust led to division and war. Eventually, one re-emerged as leader with a new name. "He was Augustus, the first emperor of the new Roman Empire[1]."

When writing about the Second Triumvirate, Donald L. Wasson interestingly pointed out that "while women were recognized as citizens in Rome, they were not permitted to participate in governmental affairs[22]." (This is reference number three below). His statement was a reminder that cultural norms of excluding women, have been engrained throughout global history. Reflection led me to a revelation that by way of an alliance encompassing negative thoughts, self-doubt, fear and hesitation, the Triumvirate has held a large segment of people back from living freely, embodying self-confidence and succeeding, due to aggrandizing hurdles in our journeys.

As women and women of color, we already have systemic barriers stacked against us due to major sectors having been established by men and for men which is evidenced by the almost invisible presence of women in high level corporate, religious, and government/political positions. When women pursue those positions, they have to possess more credentials, experience and qualifications; even so, they are still paid less wages for the same work, which has led to the gender pay gap. If securing sustainable work and pay are so difficult for one demographic group or an intersection of demographics, the system was not set up with consideration for the needs of individuals from particular demographic groups and their potential contributions were not accounted for.

---

[1] Donald L. Wasson, "Second Triumvirate," World History Encyclopedia, April 18, 2016, https://www.worldhistory.org/Second_Triumvirate/.
[2] Ibid.

We hear the concept that "representation matters" and believe it necessary for all levels of society and throughout diverse work sectors. As passionate leaders who want to forge a path for others, we concentrate on landing opportunities of influence. Sadly, reality sets in when you get to the table but colloquialisms around gender expectations trigger the Impostor Syndrome and you feel exiguous and isolated, which can minimize your very existence. My exhortation is that once you get to the table, you don't shy away from the fight; because I assure you that it will require fight to lead change. If you can tap your leadership skills, you will build credibility and influence change and break barriers for others; this can help you overcome the Impostor Syndrome.

"Representation matters" cannot just be the nice thing to say in the face of demographic shifts and new identities; this necessitates action to accompany words that will result in creating inclusive policies and practices, which are reflective of people's needs. Creating emotionally safe spaces is crucial for diverse leaders to triumph because it's tough enough to advocate for others but when you also have to battle ignorance, arrogance and intolerance to co-exist in places where you're trying to influence change, it's demoralizing. The good news is that you have the ability to make representation a reality. Can you identify how you might accomplish this?

Profundity of one's abilities, influence, and value, show up when we allow ourselves to flow in our gifts and stay receptive to wherever the journey takes us. Ever had an "aha" moment after coaching someone through a tough decision, presenting a knockout session, or reading your amazing written work where you see clearly that you were made for this and that you have greatness to share? Bottle up the forceful energy from self-validation on a victorious day so you can fuel yourself on the days when you are not as sure of yourself. Ups and downs are guaranteed in life, more so for those facing strenuous circumstances. On the bright side, difficulties bring forth an opportunity for you to strengthen yourself and shine as a solutions-oriented leader moving forward.

EXPLORING MACHISMO **AND MARIANISMO**

The Latino/Hispanic/Latinx (terms used interchangeably) culture has been scrutinized for gender expectations that push people to identify as male and female, as well as to adopt norms relating to males as strong and females as submissive. Machismo and Marianismo are terms encompassing this history and the labeling of characteristics for males and females. This delineation has contributed to maintaining the status quo in regards to gender, delaying women from pursuing public attainment and holding back the advancement of women through main stream opportunities, including receiving just payment for the work they do.

The gender pay gap exists for all women but widens for some racial and ethnic groups. For every one dollar that a White male earns, women earn as follows: Asian American, Native Hawaiian and Pacific Islander, eighty cents; White, seventy-three cents; Black, sixty-four cents; Latina, fifty-four cents; and Native American, fifty-one cents[3]. At a glance, this is just another social injustice but I pose it is an attestation of systemic patterns of abuse by men in power. When attention is drawn to misconduct, outcomes are sometimes painted as discrepancies or resulting from lack of awareness in an attempt to minimize the blatant actions to keep women limited, which have historically occurred and are still occurring. To understand why, we should identify the behavior because common language allows us to collaborate and move the needle on critical issues that demand change.

What is Machismo?[4] Machismo is defined by the Cambridge Dictionary, "Male behavior that is strong and forceful, and shows very traditional ideas

---

[3] Deborah Swerdlow, "Equal Pay Day: The Race and Gender Wage Gap," *Idealist,* Nov 1, 2023, 10:00 a.m., https://www.idealist.org/en/careers/equal-pay-day-race-gender.
[4] Machismo in English, Cambridge Dictionary, accessed January 9, 2024, https://dictionary.cambridge.org/us/dictionary/spanish-english/machismo.

about how men and women should behave." The term Machismo is traced as appearing in the dictionary in 1948 but has been used for long before that. The Spanish root word is *macho*, which is viewed as manly, tough, the boss, and head of the house. There is tension associated with being "the person in charge," so it's not always as glamorous as presented to be the *macho.* Implications of such load can involve abusing substances as a coping mechanism when it becomes too burdensome to be in charge, isolating when unable to meet the responsibilities of being the sole breadwinner, and violence in the home that has been linked to patriarchy.

What is Marianismo?[5] Marianismo is defined by the APA Dictionary of Psychology as "In many Latin American or Hispanic cultures, an idealized traditional feminine gender role characterized by submissiveness, selflessness, chastity, hyperfemininity, and acceptance of Machismo in males. Although clearly derived from the traditional ideal of the Virgin Mary, Marianismo is not to be confused with a specific religious practice of the Roman Catholic Church." The term Marianismo emerged in 1973 when Evelyn P. Stevens called attention to the behavior as the equivalent of Machismo. She was an American political scientist, professor, and author who studied, worked in, and wrote about Latin America. Her documentation and explanation of the expectations and behaviors of Latinas in an essay highlighted the first time a corresponding outline was presented. It featured the particulars of a culture where gender commands how individuals, couples, and families are portrayed to carry out responsibilities, manage family, and work, as well as interact inside and outside their homes with people from a different gender or identity.

Marianismo is based on the notion that women are sacrificial, nurturing individuals who sit at the bottom of their own priority list due to putting everyone else before themselves. An interesting theme emerged in my doctoral research titled, "A Profile of Latina Leadership in the United States" where study participants highlighted that family plays a positive role in their leadership success but also impeded their progress.

---

[5] APA Dictionary of Psychology, American Psychological Association, accessed January 19, 2024, https://dictionary.apa.org/marianismo.

Upon further analysis, this conflict makes sense in that family uplifts you and shows up for you in a way that motivates you to push yourself to succeed. On the other side of that coin, they will convict you if you can't participate in family events or live up to their expectations. The apprehension of repercussions for not showing up when loved ones expect you to, may incite you to pass up professional responsibilities. Juggling personal and professional responsibilities is tough and can take a physical, mental, and emotional toll, which I posit, is a direct result of the interconnectedness between Marianismo, the Impostor Syndrome, and Perfectionism. Contending with one of these ideals can lead to the other, causing a wave of internal doubt and distress. Recognize that trying to do everything well—all of the time—is exhausting! Have you ever felt exhausted? I sure have.

Findings from my 2011 doctoral study indicate that survey respondents highlighted thirty-six characteristics they believed effective Latina leaders should possess (See Tables 4.31 through 4.33 and Tables 4.35 through 4.38). The responses included choices from a provided list of twenty-nine characteristics, as well as nine characteristics added by respondents in the "other" category. Additionally, interviewees added another nine characteristics they believed effective Latina leaders should possess. Over three hundred and thirty-five survey respondents and four interviewees suggested that to be considered an effective Latina leader, you need to possess forty-three characteristics. Realistically, who can possess all of these characteristics to succeed in leadership and have a good footing in life without caving into the constraints? Marianismo mentality emerged throughout the study results.

Marianismo is a term used by Latinos to refer to the role of Latinas within their family, community, and society. However, when we examine gender expectations across cultural groups, we will recognize norms relating to Marianismo but may have a term for the behavior. For example, in the Asian community where women are generally reticent, they display the tendencies through reserved body language and suppression. These standards fall

under the Marianismo postulation. We cross from respectful engagements to oppression when men operate under a pretense of admiring the deity of women, yet hold them back at home, in professional spaces, and throughout society. Asian women have the smallest gender pay gap for women of color but still face workplace challenges as many are frontline and service employees. Latinas are second to lowest paid, followed by Native American women who have the largest gender pay gap. The detriment is connected to the extent that women have adopted Marianismo as a measure for their lives and acceptable compensation; such beliefs are inherited instruction throughout generations.

In recent years, we have seen a surge in writings about Marianismo, which is likely due to increased awareness by women who are accessing higher education at faster rates, seeking and landing visible roles, as well as breaking cycles that don't allow them to thrive. I first wrote about Marianismo during my doctoral studies where Latina leadership categories comprised Marianismo and New Latina: "Marianismo represents the following leadership characteristics: Compassionate, empathetic, generous, good listener, humble, sensitive, service oriented, understanding, and willing to sacrifice. New Latina represents the following leadership characteristics: Ambitious, assertive, competitive, determined, hard-working, perseverance, and self-confident."

To further explicate Latina leadership, I later coined the term Modern Marianismo in a *Huffington Post* article. Modern Marianismo is a confluence of the two leadership categories from my research that are direct depictions of the Latino (Marianismo) and American (New Latina) cultures. An experience involving reconciliation of our dual cultures. The term proposes and that one can be—and promotes that one should be—compassionate and assertive, generous and determined, humble and self-confident. Ascendancy will follow one's investment in merging the two worlds, cultures, and beliefs that sketch expectations and standards for the way women should live and lead.

WHY TALK ABOUT MARIANISMO?

This book tackles Marianismo, not just from a life perspective, but as a leadership journey in an attempt to gesture women to see themselves as leaders and associate appropriately relating to behaviors and language. Leadership is about authorizing yourself and others, which is what we witness when we examine how women live. The distinction in demeanor is whether a woman embraces herself as a leader or not and how she acts upon her convictions.

Sometimes people believe in us more than we believe in ourselves because we spend more time questioning our abilities and hesitating to take action in various areas of our lives than we do fostering our talents. If you have the good fortune of having loved ones who believe in you, let them guide you away from the bondage of the Impostor Syndrome. Leaving behind the self-doubt will enable you move into self-empowerment knowing that you are smart enough for your assignment, brave enough for your fight, and proficient enough to reach those who need to receive your message because you are a leader. Do you self-identify as a leader?

Connecting to leadership as a way of life and to the principles that guide masterful leadership provides women and Black, Indigenous, and people of color (BIPOC) leaders with a foundation for tackling the challenges they face. Such exploration is motivation for considering a simpler, user-friendly framework for empowering individuals to see themselves from an angle of strength, personal might and possessing the capacity to positively influence others—even when challenged.

Often times, people want you to tell them what they want to hear, even if it is not what they need to hear. You have a choice and responsibility to be honest with those you care about in order to support them living out their

destiny and taking care of themselves. Honesty is a necessary trait for good leadership and building strong relationships; but it's tough to hold steadfast with those who do not appreciate you telling the truth. Hence why women tend to sugar coat the truth to maintain peace.

Peacemaking over truth-telling is typical behavior for Marianistas, who prefer avoiding hurt. But the truth will fester, which can build resentment and cause distance instead of trust. When women do speak truthfully, they receive insults like she is bitchy, bossy, and arrogant. You have to let the negativity roll off your back and not fall into the trap of cynicism. Speak up knowing in your heart that you're contributing to the betterment of people and society, especially speaking truth to power to disturb the status quo. Whether good or bad, emotions and thoughts occupy our time and energy.

Access permits something or someone entrance to our life, mind, feelings and decisions, which makes it a priceless commodity that we should not easily give away. Coming from big families and/or communities where everyone collaborates can blind us to the essence of protecting ourselves by limiting access. Marianismo alludes to a free-for-all mien, which seeds one's vulnerability to destructive people, toxic environments, and dangerous behaviors. This will drain your energy, waste your time, and restrict your productivity in areas that should matter most. The common denominator in the list of loss, is you. As long as you allow it, people will take and borrow from you without reciprocating. You can acquire a transformational leadership mentality which appeals for you to re-examine and establish criteria for what motivates you and others to move along in their respective paths.

Choice is a privilege you deserve but must protect to stay in control of your destiny and life while you work to make the world a better place. You can elect who to grant your time and energy to, who you will listen to, whose practices to follow, and whose presence to be in because exposure determines your path. If exposed to positive people and content, your frame of mind will be hopeful and affirming. If exposed to negative people and

content, you will be pessimistic and situations will seem bleak. Have you ever found yourself in this predicament? If so, how did you surpass it?

Hesitation about choice is connected to humility, which may cause us to relinquish delineations that seem harsh or require us to say the bad word no; because as Marianistas, we place the feelings and needs of others before our own. It is interesting how that word is spelled and means the same in English and Spanish. Let's add *no más* (no more) to the bad word glossary; because it is time to trample on the cycles that force you into the Triumvirate. Self-reflection presents an opportunity to check in with yourself regularly to work through this new practice of turning away from the habit of always saying yes.

As hard as it is to say no or share honest sentiments with people, we must stick to our word once we say something; because it's verification of our integrity and makes us stronger. Efficacious leaders cannot speak from different places; you must say what you mean and mean what you say even if your perspective is unpopular and sets you apart from everyone else. We ought to accept affirming and dismissive reactions on how we show up because we cannot control others' emotions and trying to do so falls within Perfectionism norms.

Part of navigating these engagements well is to prepare to stay away when the vibe is not in your favor. Women are expected to always be present and available like the image portrayed in movies and mainstream media that grandmothers are always waiting to care for and serve their loved ones, near and extended, to the neighborhood, church, and community. I pose the image of a grandma, whose family joins when she is delivering a keynote speech in a room filled with high level executives, or partakes in an author's launch event, where she is featured, or watches her news interview. Why not see and feature women in the forefront instead of on the sidelines?

We must venture to shift the dynamics of womanhood to showcase the skills, strength, and contributions of amazing women across the globe.

Aspiring to carry out the attributes of strong leadership will serve as a guide for their purpose-fulfilling journey of contributing to much needed change, at any level of society that they feel called to penetrate. This process is how one can move away from grappling with the Impostor Syndrome, fighting guilt from the Marianismo ideal, and struggling with imperfection—to operating intentionally as a transformational leader moving with purpose instead of from hesitation.

Transformative experiences impact us as individuals and a collective society. Over the past decade, we've seen an increase of publications by women and Latinas telling their stories. Stories that were tough to live are the hardest to share but those touch people deeply while freeing authors from pain, fear, and sadness.

Storytelling is a multifaceted tool that can help break generational cycles, develop young leaders, and record changes in history, whether good or bad. Such a tool can create a pathway from Marianismo to Modern Marianismo, because telling your story allows you to take your power back from life's circumstances and from people who have hurt you. Writing one's own narrative is an empowering experience that can free you from self-doubt, discomfort of living an imperfect life, and the feeling of being an impostor in your own life.

EFFECTS OF **THE IMPOSTOR SYNDROME**

The Impostor Syndrome[6] was introduced in 1978 by Dr. Pauline Clance and Dr. Suzanne Imes to explain the experiences of their clients who were winning but struggling to acknowledge their triumph. They were confronted with the struggle of working so hard to gain perceived success, but then they were unable to embrace and celebrate their victories and faced an uphill internal war with themselves. For individuals from backgrounds posing additional hurdles—such as economic, racial or ethnic, and family dynamics, among many possible indicators of stress—the strife is exacerbated, causing a prison within their minds that inhibits progress even when they have the title and status to ascend.

A crucial area to ruminate on is: How do you define success and will you embrace it when you achieve it? Self-doubt tends to override celebration of success, an aspect of the Impostor Syndrome, which is a self-defeating behavior, thwarting someone from progressing, and stepping into purpose. Having the right people in your personal and professional circles will help to strengthen you to see more clearly what you cannot see when you're overwhelmed and grappling with emotions.

A major negative effect of the Impostor Syndrome is how it relates to your emotional and mental health. You have to find your power and move in it; sometimes taking it back from yourself if you have suppressed it by falling prey to the debilitating implications of not feeling worthy or strong. Approaches to crush the negativity can arise from a standpoint of spirituality and/or personal development.

Recently, I've heard many inspirational and spiritual talks referring to

---

6 Machismo in English. Cambridge Dictionary, accessed January 19, 2024, https://dictionary.cambridge.org/us/dictionary/spanish-english/Marianista.

a battle of the mind and I realize that, at face value, this is a taboo topic. People don't want to talk about mental health because there has been a negative connotation associated with this aspect of life. However, it is a very real and necessary discussion and we have to help people reconcile so many things they are juggling, as well as the emotions and thoughts that come with the mental health journey.

Overwhelming stressors lead to physical and mental health implications, such as heart disease, high blood pressure, digestive issues and depression, among many. When not feeling well, one cannot be their best in any capacity, which is a caveat to the challenges we are addressing. Sadly, this outcome is too common because of the extensive to-do lists between our home, work, community, and spiritual commitments. The American Psychological Association warns about the gravity of possible side effects and advises that, in addition to stress management, you increase positive activities and emotions to counter the worrisome. Attention to our well-being is crucial for advancing in each area of our lives.

We are living in a time where people from any age can experience mental health struggles—from students to stay-at-home parents to executives—which is impacting families, communities, and the workplace in general that cause scary situations to occur. As leaders, we can tap our resilience, faith or spiritual grounding, and desire for meaningful changes to enhance the greater good.

strive for progress
NOT PERFECTION

PERFECTION **DOESN'T EXIST**

Perfectionism is a topic studied widely pertaining to leadership, health, religion, and people focused facets. ". . . Refers to the tendency to set excessively high standards for oneself and others."[7] The intent of being good at everything and doing all things well is ingrained in the mind and habits of individuals trying to meet unachievable supposition of perfection. What transpires is this person always being on, unable to turn off because they need to be in control to ensure their highest standards are successfully met. Journalist and Activist Gloria Steinem said, "Perfectionism is internalized oppression."[8]

The discussion about perfectionism is traced back to the 1800s by theorists Alfred Adler and Karen Horney. Perfectionists have been the center of studies for many years; researchers have sought to shed light on the characteristics displayed, as well as the root causes and implications of the mindset. The phenomenon has been reviewed from religious, psychological, trauma, educational and political aspects, in an attempt to explicate the positive and negative associations. It's worth noting that superiority and inferiority tie into a way of life targeting perfection, two sides of the same coin. Superiority is about extending to the highest level, being the best, and validating your self-worth, synonymous with perfection. Inferiority is about feelings of inadequacy, dissatisfaction even when investing your best, and giving credence to low self-esteem.

---

[7] Laura Dorwart, "Understanding the Psychology behind Perfectionism," Verywell Health, accessed January 12, 2024, https://www.verywellhealth.com/perfectionism-5323816#:~:text=Perfectionism%20is%20defined%20as%20the,%2C%20and%20unattainable%20goal%2Dsetting.

[8] Vix Anderton, "29 Quotes about Perfectionism to Change Your Perspective," LinkedIn, February 20, 2023, https://www.linkedin.com/pulse/29-quotes-perfectionism-change-your-perspective-vix-anderton-frsa.

Ever wonder why people approach you about their needs, what promotes requests of you, or which traits captivate them to want to be like you? Give thought to how you make life, leading and producing look easy and attainable. Lots of people have told me they were inspired to tackle big tasks due to my successful doctoral journey, where I completed an accelerated program while working full time and having twins. Looking back on that time in my life does make me proud of my accomplishments, but it also reminds me that my health suffered at the cost of too many demands and how I wanted to give up many times along the way.

People may think you do not get weak and cannot fathom that you might break down because they envision you on a pedestal of non-stop moving and doing since that is the side of you that they usually see. Reality is that we all get tired and need to be aware of where we will find strength to keep going. My resurgence comes from drawing upon my faith; partnership and love from my husband who is self-identified and proven to be my number one fan; encouragement from family, friends, colleagues and followers; as well as modeling the vitality of role models.

Old sayings get passed on, which are sometimes incorrect notions. For example, I beg to differ with the tagline we have repeated for years that "practice makes perfect." Yes, we surely need to practice in order to improve, but we should start saying that "practice makes better," because it won't make us perfect. I do agree with passing along the message, "No one is perfect." Repeating this often can remove the stigma that we are supposed to be.

SURVIVING INTERCONNECTED **IDEOLOGIES**

Examine the long list of demands for your time and energy such as trying to take care of the needs of people in your life from kids to partner to colleagues, serving on organizational boards, volunteering in your community, participating in spiritual and/or educational activities. How much time is left to take care of your own needs and pursue desires?

Hence why I don't believe in balance. How can I do everything well? The pressure of trying to be good at all things on a regular basis—is a heavy burden which perpetuates perfectionist expectations for me, by me, and by others. We are bombarded with messages of how we're supposed to behave, obligations to deliver, and who should approve of us. If internalized, these patterns stemming from Marianismo can cause us to second-guess our goals, accomplishments, and way of life. This leads to attempted perfection and when unachieved, instigates the impostor feelings. The three ideologies are interconnected, which is why we feel unraveled but can't seem to grasp the specific cause.

Concerns and doubts escalate when challenges arise that are beyond our control. Ever experience betrayal, feeling undervalued or unseen? When we put all of our energy, time, and effort into something that we're confident will make a difference but we experience negativity from those we invested in, we might feel defeated. At times, life might feel like you're taking one step forward and five steps backwards. People will betray and disappoint us, which is tough for perfectionists to submit to since they aim to check all the boxes and anticipate that others will do the same.

However, we cannot fall into Perfectionism in trying to please others; because it's not possible to please everyone. Why do we try so hard to please others even at the cost of our own happiness? Women are perceived

as nurturing and thrive on building fruitful relationships which is connected to wanting to be on good terms with everyone. This is the Marianista way. We envision driving change by engaging a broader audience, but there is no way to guarantee full buy-in from others. Resistance causes us to question if we have a clear vision, encourages us to shrink in spaces we should be dominating and oppugn our purpose, leaving us to feel as though we are impostors.

However, one cannot allow the vicious cycle to force us to waiver on our values, issues we care about or our self-worth. Give yourself time and permission to grieve and feel the emotions from negative experiences; but then, pick yourself up and re-energize so you can assess how to best use your gifts and choose which people and efforts you'll commit to. Dismantling the ideologies holding you captive is the key to freedom, but it takes ongoing and concerted effort.

Self-care is essential to surviving life's challenges and can be a strategy for healing and refueling from pain, grief, betrayal, and burnout. Allowing yourself the space to unplug from routines, responsibilities and even people, can draw a line in the sand to ensure your survival. Allow yourself to accept that you deserve to take a break; that it's OK to have fun; and you can respond no to asks that you cannot meet or are misaligned from your current priorities.

Sometimes the idea of not being active every moment feels like laziness or like we can't afford it because we've had to work harder than others to be at the same tables, and we're used to moving at a fast pace. However, periods of inactivity will allow one to refocus, rest the mind and body, and draw upon new ideas that emerge when we declutter internally, which will enable us to be more effective upon returning to our duties.

REDEFINING GENDER **EXPECTATIONS**

Paradigm shifts require knowledge of history and consequences for specific groups to learn how we can improve conditions for marginalized communities. In this context, we're referring to female-identifying individuals who've been boxed into careers portrayed as feminine, such as teaching or administrative roles.

We need male figures in such roles to bring diversity of views and experiences. But work sector norms engendered these professions to be associated with emotion and a tenderness attributed to femininity, which made it difficult for men to enter some sectors without being singled out or labeled as feminine.

Labeling has always existed from the U.S. Census using categories for people to select their racial and ethnic groups to employers wanting to understand who is in their workforce. While labeling might be a helpful methodology for data collection, it's divisive as people try to fit into certain categories or separate themselves as superior to other groups.

When we approach day-to-day tasks relating to home, work, and community, we may not realize in the moment that we're operating on auto pilot. We move in tradition and norms without acknowledging the external indicators for why and how we do things. For example, when I'm preparing to travel for business and know that I will be leaving my home and my family, I move frantically to clean every part of my house, handle all the laundry, cook several meals, and leave everything in place.

My husband is a great partner who can handle all family and home matters without my assistance, and he reminds me that all will be well whether I finish everything or not. However, I'm not comfortable leaving without being sure that every item on my to-do list is checked off. The thought of not finishing things causes feelings of anxiety and incompleteness.

In mulling over on the circumstances impacting my behaviors and feelings, I can pinpoint fear of inadequacy and worry of not being the best mother and wife when I pursue my professional endeavors. It's as though fulfilling one role well, means that I cannot fulfill the others, which are also in high regard for me. The perception that one should choose between managing responsibilities of the hats we wear and our ambitions—to access professional opportunities, increase visibility for enhancement of your public depiction, secure mainstream leadership—is at the root of an unnecessary psychological load we carry, leading to feelings of deficiency and guilt.

Emotional baggage ranges for individuals based on family history, medical issues, experiencing poverty, trauma, abuse, or grief and any unresolved experience that has taken root in the soul. When bogged down by life, our focus is not on moving forward, and one certainly cannot lead adequately amidst such burdens. Marianismo would find you with a coerced smile, trying to help others while your heart aches when pondering your own options. The Impostor Syndrome would produce shame from being unable to keep up with the poundage like someone in your position should. Perfectionism would usher you to burnout due to exhaustion from dealing with personal conflicts and those of others. Finding yourself at a crossroad, the choice is between giving in or putting forth the effort to ameliorate chaos.

DEVELOPING **YOUR IDENTITY**

Machismo, Marianismo, the Impostor Syndrome and Perfectionism ideologies can take root at a young age based on a child's environment and the adults they engage with. Our identity formation can be positively or negatively influenced by trusting what is passed onto us. This is why raising children and working with young people is a monumental responsibility. Adults can plant seeds of positivity, hope, and unity or negativity, hopelessness, and discord based on their lived experiences and how they choose to view the world, social issues, and people. Youth is susceptible. So, we ought to be mindful that unrealistic demands placed on them and whether they are encouraged or berated, will have a critical impact in their evolution.

Development of our identity is also by effected aspects ranging from physical attributes, which can cause us to feel good about ourselves or be self-conscious; how we dress, which can categorize us; the way we speak, which may raise questions from others, etc. A pivotal aspect of identity development relates to our moral compass, which is greatly informed by adults in our lives who provide a foundation for how we see the world and interact with others.

Many cultural norms have been passed to us and we pass them to the next generation, at times not realizing that we're sustaining antiquated views on life, people, and leadership. Negative cycles can stem from unwritten laws, such as financial obligations prioritized before education, religious practices above personal customs, and family commitments taking precedence over professional endeavors. An antipathetic outlook on generational cycles that hold people captive is a source for the inability to progress, leading to an identity crisis, which opens the door to manipulation by the interconnected ideological cycle of the Triumvirate.

"There are four key personal/internal factors of identity: perceptions, attitudes, values, and beliefs."[9] These factors frame the way we view people and behaviors, what we do and don't acquiesce to, and how we rationalize boundaries for ourselves and others. Such parameters inform our identity and how we lead. We continue to evolve based on these guides; therefore, we can reject parameters that are more hindrance than motivators.

Surrendering to tension and worry will cue anxiety, uncertainty, and self-doubt. By taking time alone to rest, deliberate, and fully process the existent, you can conquer the despair and gain revelation. It is a beautiful encounter for the switch to flip and you receive a download of clarity on maneuvering what is at hand. Will you make a decision to proceed with full force or shift direction based on new understanding you have acquired? It is healthy to go through this exchange within yourself to evaluate emotions, expectations, and opposition that if not regulated; and it will open the door to the Triumvirate.

Active advocacy to reverse the Marianismo mentality can be for oneself but also for people we are connected to. At times, we don't realize that we are stuck in a behavior pattern hindering progress; so, if you care about someone and notice they are a Marianista, you should share your concerns with them. Approach gingerly for a fruitful exchange, keep the discussion centered on specific actions and progression.

My *abuela* recognized the Marianista in me and tried to steer me away from the tendencies. Having lost her mother when she was eight years old, she was one of two girls. But her older sister had epilepsy, so she inherited looking after her family, doing chores, and ultimately serving as the matriarch. At this tender age, children should be having fun and learning new things instead of being overburdened with caregiving and tasks that replace the spark of innocence with the troubles of life. She carried out those duties for a decade before she married my grandfather and started a family. I was blessed to be raised by my maternal grandparents to help me through the tragedy of my mother's early death. I learned so much from their tenacity and regrets.

---

[9] Anonymous. "Factors Shaping an Identity: Internal & External," Study.com, accessed January 12, 2024, https://study.com/academy/lesson/factors-influencing-identity-formation.html.

One thing my grandmother instilled in me was to do everything she did not have a chance to—from traveling to accessing education and having a fruitful career to permitting public spotlighting of my gifts. When she noticed my Marianista behaviors, she encouraged me to take credit for my work, nudged me to chase the next level even when I did not feel I was ready, and elicited in me the demand for merited honor for my hard work, dedication, and skills. Everything she set me up for came from the deficits in her life that she did not want me to repeat. Often solidifying the seeds that she planted in me with comments like, "if I was educated" or "if I had a chance to travel" and alluding to that alternative life as exceptional compared the one she lived. Living vicariously through me, her name's sake, she would dress up to join me at luncheons and used the bullhorn at political events—a true testament to stepping into greatness at any age, even with regrets about not having accessed or accomplished more.

UNDERSTANDING **MODERN MARIANISMO**

It is interesting that desire can be viewed negatively, as if you're aspiring to something sinful by wanting to climb the success ladder. Desire is driven by passion for things we enjoy, which aligns with pursuing one's purpose. When we reframe how words are used and viewed, we can move away from judgement and push forward towards progress that can indisputably impact many people. The push and pull between expectations imposed by others—those we have self-imposed and our new frame of thinking and living through a freedom of choice lens—is how we can break away from traditional Marianismo and move into Modern Marianismo.

"You may be wondering what Modern Marianismo looks like. From accessing higher education and technical vocations, to being super mom, to having careers that were not typical for women/women of color, to accepting leadership roles in various areas of their lives, Latinas are changing the world."[10]

Modern Marianismo is an ongoing process, the freedom to define yourself as a woman and live in that frame of mind. Modern Marianismo is not just about stepping away from the traditional cultural and/or religious expectations but more so about choosing the aspects of those norms which resonate with your desires and goals. Progression involves reconciling how your preferred convictions will drive your behaviors such as what you will or won't tolerate from others, clarifying your expectations in relationships, and pinpointing what you will pursue in life to appraise yourself successful. Modern Marianismo is specifically about leadership—seeing yourself as a leader, self-identifying as a leader in every aspect of your life, and pursuing your best leadership experience because you deserve it and everyone around you will benefit from your feat.

---

[10] Damary Bonilla-Rodriguez, "Latinas and Modern Marianismo," *HuffPost*, December 25, 2013, https://www.huffpost.com/entry/latinas-and-modern-marianismo_b_4165200.

A distinguishing facet of Modern Marianismo entails embarking on a process of deep internal exploration, coupled with determination to flourish in your own right and faithful implementation of the following tenets to guide your moral compass. They are:

- values you want to consent to, promote and live by;
- decisions that will ensure you live and lead authentically;
- how you choose to identify and be identified in the various roles you hold;
- ways you want to positively impact the spaces you occupy.

Once you realize the aspects obstructing you from performing at your full potential, you have to commit to standing firm in the truth of who you choose to be. I know firsthand that claiming your rightful place in leadership and welcoming visibility for your efforts isn't always comfortable. But growth as a person and as a leader requires willingness to take charge.

The analogy of a blooming flower comes to mind. Starting with a seed, then a bud, and finally full-blown beauty that brightens up lives. Success lies in the process of watering, exposing to light, and giving care to the plant. In this same manner, leaders will bloom if we nurture the seed of greatness inside of ourselves and those around us. This is especially true for cultivating young leaders. If it is challenging for adults to manage leadership, it's tougher for youth who are still developing a sense of self.

Early development is when to invest time and resources to guiding youth in understanding they have a special place in the world. Thought partnership with them can establish a perspective that they don't have to be perfect because it's not achievable. But confirming their hard work and determination will ensure leaving a mark in spaces they will occupy. It's never too early for young people to invest in themselves; they should aim to learn from the experiences of women around them, build awareness of possible disputes they will face based on who they are, and commit to a path of leadership success by way of *mentorship, allyship,* and *scholarship*.

Culture is an accumulation of many layers inclusive of passing down traditions, years of practices, and expressions of values we consent to and promulgate. Demographic representation ties into culture around messages about what we should believe and how we should behave. Hence why Marianismo, the Impostor Syndrome and Perfectionism strike women from all backgrounds. There are ranges to effects of the Triumvirate based on how your cultural universe regards women.

OVERCOMING **THE TRIUMVIRATE**

Our mind is the most powerful tool to overcome the Triumvirate because everything we do or don't do, comes from our mental determination of feelings and actions. Speaking about something is a great way to get going and writing it out will assist in visualizing the outcome. But when you think about how to make it happen, your mental fortitude will dictate how you feel and what actions (if any) will take place. In order to make fruitful decisions and tackle the tests before you, thoughts ought to be free from self-doubt and deteriorating attitudes so you can march in authority as the person who controls your path.

Difficulties are a given in life but can be reframed as opportunities so as not to remain stuck in what you cannot change. It is time to break generational cycles by educating ourselves on where we have picked up these ideals for expectations, who has impacted our views about how we should behave, and take the reins of our lives and leadership journey. Along the way, demystifying perfection for our children and youth. Self-doubt has plagued generations of families from all racial and ethnic backgrounds, adding detriment to families facing socioeconomic and demographic related disparities.

When we make a conscious decision to not promote negative cycles, not pass along our burdens to the next generation, instead to view experiences through an action centered lens—we are more likely to overcome the difficulties before us. It is time to take the reins of life and leadership at the level that you desire, whether at home, local community, or global society. There is a need for your voice. Steer away from traditional, cultural, and gender setbacks and step into your greatness.

Maneuvering unequivocally through adversities entails one accessing encouraging language, relevant information and aspirations to move in a constructive direction. I present several pathways to reframing your approach, keep in mind that this is about you and that is copacetic. You cannot not diminish your brilliance for any reason.

WORK THROUGH VULNERABILITY

Allowing ourselves to be vulnerable might be tough since the transparency can be interpreted as weakness. Perceived weakness goes hand in hand with low self-confidence and can prompt criticism, which perpetuates the Triumvirate. I pose that vulnerability is not a bad characteristic because allowing yourself to be vulnerable is acknowledging that you are not good at everything. It can release you from the weight of your own expectations and those of others. Honestly, authorship pushed me to vulnerably admit that I was not sure I could deliver the greatness expected from me. I pride myself on giving my all to everything I do, which often results in reactions and requests for more —content, involvement, time with people, etc.

When I've talked with people about writing, they've encouraged me and shared anticipated outcomes from my work. When I started writing and creating content, the doubts crept in about whether I can contribute substantive value to my sphere of work. To ground myself, I have re-read previous contributions and amaze myself with the relevant work produced. You may see someone as successful but they can experience self-doubt that holds them back. Hence the need to admit when we struggle, share with those we believe we can reach and push through the opposition.

The responsibility of leading can be lonely and, at times, things may appear gloomy. You find yourself needing and seeking motivation on those tough days and feeling unsure of where it will come from. Truthfully, motivation can be found in obvious or unexpected ways, such as coming across an inspirational post online, hearing something on the radio or television that makes your heart skip a bit, or reading text that causes your soul to leap. Even exposure to people who hate you, can propel you to the next level. Stay open minded to receiving from people, places and things that will uplift you and commission your creativity to flow.

You have to control your narrative and not let someone else create it for you. How you view yourself, your struggles, and your approach to resolution will put you on a path to strengthening and elevating your leadership platform.

IDENTIFY WITH TRANSFORMATIONAL LEADERSHIP

Seizing the moments to bring about better conditions in diverse spaces, can be an approach to working through the internal clash of the Triumvirate. I often say that it is sometimes easier for me to fight for others than it is to fight for myself. If this applies, then we can draw upon our eagerness to help others and the devotion we have to creating a better world as walking into our purpose and attainment of self-worth.

According to Langston.edu, "Transformational leadership is defined as a leadership approach that causes change in individuals and social systems. In its ideal form, it creates valuable and positive change in the followers with the end goal of developing followers into leaders."

Transformational leaders are driven by the vision of influencing and motivating others, promoting advancement together, and growing individuals from followers to leaders. The description is how passionate people see the world; it is having a cup half full mentality versus seeing the cup as half empty.

Successfully navigating the Triumvirate requires you to hone in on your life and leadership ideals. My personal mantra is that exposure equals access. This rings true for me because I was born into unfavorable statistics of poverty, a teen mother who died at age twenty-seven, wasn't in contact with my father and grew up in less than desirable means which was a desolate path. Through exposure to mentors who poured into me, continued education to stretch my mind, a faith foundation to keep me grounded, and the support of loved ones to keep me focused, I was able to access meaningful work. I earned a good living and gained tools to learn how to advocate for myself and others, so I could be the change agent tugging at me in the face of injustice. Keep in mind that we never arrive in our leadership journey; we must continue exposing ourselves to knowledge, people and activities that will allow for our growth, breaking and building, inspiration and consistent upward and onward movement.

ACCEPT PARTNERSHIP

If you are blessed enough to have a partner, allow them to share responsibilities. Sometimes we get stuck in the world of Marianismo and we do not welcome the contributions of those around us. I have always traveled for work, which has precipitated different reactions from family, friends and colleagues. Some have encouraged me to pursue my efforts to develop leaders and fight for social justice while others have questioned how I can fulfill my wife and motherly duties, such as cooking from scratch and attending to my home. Conflicting messages from loved ones has caused a debate in my mind about my competence to succeed at home and work, which provoked me to question myself and experience the Triumvirate.

Fortunately, my husband has been encouraging in my pursuits of higher education to managing home and work alongside me. There have been many times during the twenty-seven years we have been together where he has reminded me that I don't have to do everything alone and that he can handle cooking, cleaning, and caring for our sons.

If you are blessed to have a partner, allow them to carry the weight with you. You should not compel yourself to bear the load alone and go down the dark path of the Triumvirate. If you are without a partner or a single mother, lean on your chosen community for encouragement, consent to childcare when offered by trusted people, and embrace the ups and downs that are the reality of life.

As my husband often reminds me, you cannot make everyone happy. The beauty of this journey is arriving at a place where you choose to make yourself happy so you can put your best effort into each day and yield to each day looking different based on what is in front of you.

TAP YOUR SPIRITUAL BELIEFS

For individuals with a spiritual foundation, it is relatively easy to connect this journey to Peter's experience of walking on water. While he watched Jesus, he succeeded but failed as soon as he turned his sight to what was humanly impossible. I want to clarify that I'm not pushing religion because legalism can increase the stressors you are already grappling with, exacerbate unrealistic expectations for women, and further marginalize communities that don't fit in a box created by the same men who don't believe women should lead.

If you do practice a religion, there are ways to navigate the structures to satisfy what you believe is assigned to you. For example, humility is highly regarded in religion and in communities of color. At face value, this trait keeps you quiet, submissive and distant from public spotlight, which is Marianismo. The ideal carries a spiritual connotation about women as a supreme being in comparison to the Virgin Mary from Catholicism. You can remain humble without being subservient.

Divinity is another religious concept connected to women as supreme beings. Described as angelic and beyond the capabilities of humanity, one can adopt this as it relates to how we are perceived by others but maintaining awareness that it's an invitation for people expecting you to be their savior which is not manageable, even for Mary. Ponder on the Bible referring to Mary as preferred amid many women and think for a moment of the burden Mary carried for being chosen for the spiritually divine task as a young, unmarried woman. Ultimately, she surrendered to her calling but realized she needed God's help to see it through. You can accept the magnitude of your life's purpose without succumbing to fulfilling it alone.

The emotions and fears many of us feel to be the first and only one when we secure positions of power or move into the public light, hurl us into combating hesitation because we're being pushed out of our comfort zones and we don't have examples of how to succeed in those spaces. For me, writing and publishing have been daunting because no one in my family had

accomplished this level and I did not want to take something from someone or promote myself so as not to appear arrogant. Even after conducting and publishing my doctoral research, earning the highest educational credentials from an accredited university, having national leadership recognition, I hesitated to expand my body of work. Ironically, people have used my/others' work and received more visibility and credit than the creator. How can you get through similar obstacles to feel confident in your abilities?

Changing your outlook will energize your forward momentum. Realizing the necessity to build upon data and resources to understand and address social justice, academic, health, and other issues we are trying to improve, positions use of one's work as integral. So, I focused on drawing from over a decade of practice since publishing my research to elevate what I started in my doctoral journey; because while I put forth time and energy to assist others, I cannot be everywhere at once. Yet, my documented work can reach many people simultaneously.

We do good work in the shadows to abide by humility, feel included, and be a team player. In fact, the world misses out when we don't contribute in ways we should because each of us has gifts that reach people differently, even when discussing the same topics. I believe in a middle ground, a humble confidence that stems from your intention; personal strength not inhibited by the reactions of others since their intent is unknown and irrelevant to your purpose. Grounding yourself this way will lead you to discern that not every opportunity is a good one and decide that you can pass up anything that is not beneficial to your advancement.

This discussion is about spirituality in terms of asserting to the existence of a higher power that encourages faith, hope, and love to light up this dark world we are living in. For me, that higher power is the God of the Bible, who I've had a personal relationship with since losing my mother to homicide when I was eight years old. The Bible talks about freedom. But how can we be free if we are chained by unrealistic expectations, venturing towards perfection, and trying to please so many people? On days when I'm unsure of myself, my sight turns to God, my husband, and my sons—all refuel me and remind me of the value I bring to every space I occupy and that my passion is to be a voice for many. Be sure to place more importance and sight on who and what will guide you through struggles and enable you to succeed.

GIVE YOURSELF GRACE

In actuality, while you can't do everything at once, you can do everything you want to do in life. My admonition, based on the context provided, is to do things at a reasonable pace and allow yourself the grace to pivot, mess up, and decide that you no longer want to do something. Writing those words was tough for me since I have not always allowed myself the flexibility to be imperfect and not to adhere to standards ingrained in me by others.

However, this book is an appeal to myself and to you—that we live life to the fullest by reconceiving what we have been taught so we can elevate ourselves and support others in their elevation. Consider that even using the word "elevate" relating to ourselves is frowned upon because it's self-serving. Ask yourself, "What is wrong with serving myself when I serve everyone else and am encouraged to do so?"

This reflective experience brought me to an interesting realization about the difference between helping someone and supporting them in relation to Marianismo, although the words are synonymous. Contemplate that culturally, help tends to address pressing needs and can be linked to dependency while support entails providing guidance and tasking someone with improving their circumstances. In both cases you would aid loved ones but it's necessary to distinguish the extent to which you will carry others' burdens.

Life is hard enough when you have to juggle your many responsibilities and expectations; adding the issues of others makes the pressure unbearable, causing you self-doubt and guilt. Eliminating relative feelings and ending the vicious pattern of compromising your well-being will depend on your ability to set standards around your capacity, clearly communicating the boundaries you've set and sticking to your decisions.

Your journey to freedom from expectations set by yourself and others, will not be easy. Successfully navigating the fear, self-doubt and judgement you will grapple with along the road to embracing your power, will depend on your devotion to self-actualization and empowerment. To get you started, I propose a 3-step contemplative, action-based holistic approach to embracing Modern Marianismo:

1. *Build up your spirit through introspection.* Contemplate who are you now and resolve who you want to become. This part of your journey will require a growth mindset.

    Resources:
    - Article: "A Growth Mindset is a Must-Have—These Thirteen Tips Will Grow Yours" by Maggie Wool.
    - Video: "Developing a Growth Mindset with Carol Dweck."
    - Book: "The Seven Habits of Highly Effective People: Powerful Lessons in Personal Change" by Stephen R. Covey.

2. *Reaffirm your identity.* Authenticate your convictions, values, and character. This part of your journey will require grounding yourself in the essence of ingenuousness.

    Resources:
    - Article: "Here's How Your Personal Identity and Sense of Self Affect Your Growth" by Heather Cherry.
    - Video: "Is Your Identity Given or Created?" by Marcus Lyon.
    - Book: "Identity: Discover Who You Are and Live a Life of Purpose." by T.D. Jakes

3. Step into your power and influence capacity. Declare your strength and uniqueness and determine how you will share your passions and talents with the world. This part of your journey will require giving credence to your innate gifts and tapping your fortitude.

    Resources:
    - Article: "How to Unlock Your Natural Gifts to Achieve Your Big Dreams" by Neel Raman.
    - Video: "How to Step into Your Power" by Lisa Nichols.
    - Book: "Now, Discover Your Strengths" by Marcus Buckingham and Donald O. Clifton, Ph.D.

THE MARIANISMO **ANTHEM**

In this written journey, we reviewed historical context of the negative influence that societal expectations have had on women and marginalized people, by default glancing at the power possessed by men and those with privilege. We delved into cultural aspects to understand the roots of leadership challenges faced by women, women of color, Latinas and all who can identify with being limited by chauvinistic views, impacted by oppressive practices, and hindered by reliance on weighted presumptions. Such discussion is especially relevant for those in the corporate, religious, and government/political sectors, where a pervasive culture of sexism, misogyny, and isms has long been accepted and anyone with family history of subjugation to male dominance and unreasonable demands.

Talented, smart, passionate individuals have been held back for too long and stuck in generational cycles of self-doubt, which thrusts one into the Triumvirate. Once practicing self-sabotaging behaviors, it becomes harder to break away and live authentically. However, the quest for justice and equity is moving in the right direction as we shed light on the causes of indignities and solutions for course correction in favor of suppressed individuals, undervalued populations, and advance the greater good.

How do we move the needle in our favor instead of watching ourselves being victimized by people who don't have our best interest as a priority? First, one can assess any situation that isn't working for them and determine what are the factors preventing progress. Next, outlining possible action steps to combat the identified obstacles. Followed by drawing upon our network to select those individuals that would be allies in creating forward momentum for ourselves and causes of importance to us. Holding a strategy meeting to thought partner on timing and enhancing your actions outline will put things in motion.

The goal is to take charge of our lives, operate within our gifts, and create the impetus for proceeding with purpose. Embarking on a personal journey of self-discovery, transformation, and development of your impenetrable spirit, you will break free from the bondage of expectations. Living carte blanche increases self-confidence authorizing you change the dynamics in spaces you occupy, and influence others to chase their own prominence. In the words of Rigoberta Menchú Tum, "I am like a drop of water on a rock. After drip, drip, dripping in the same place, I begin to leave a mark. . . ."[11] Now forge ahead to seize mastery over your thoughts, desires and decisions—propelling yourself to happiness, growth, and success because you deserve the best in life.

---

[11] Anonymous. "30 Best Rigoberta Menchu Quotes with Image," Bookey, September 13, 2023, https://www.bookey.app/quote-author/rigoberta-menchu.

ABOUT THE AUTHOR

Dr. Damary M. Bonilla-Rodriguez is a national leading authority on leadership development, especially as it pertains to diversity and inclusion. She delivers keynote addresses and presentations drawing upon her experience from roles in the non-profit, private, and government/political sectors, as well as her doctoral research. Her research about Latina leadership in the United States has served as the foundation for events, conference sessions, publications, and content development—to address the urgency of leadership development for a fast-growing population and create a pipeline of diverse leaders.

Dr. Bonilla-Rodriguez holds a Bachelor of Arts degree in Spanish and Social Work from the College of New Rochelle, where she received the College President's Medal, graduated with departmental honors, and was awarded the Sigma Delta Pi Spanish Award. She also holds a Master of Science degree in Organizational Communications and a Specialized Certification in Corporate Communications, both from the College of New Rochelle. Personal endeavors of overcoming statistics and accessing higher education, led her to earn a Doctorate in Education focusing on Executive Leadership from St. John Fisher College. She self-identifies as a lifelong learner and recently completed the Harwood Institute's Coaching program.

To change the political and leadership landscape for Latinos, Dr. Bonilla-Rodriguez ran for state representative in the 189th District of Pennsylvania in 2016, where she became the first Hispanic to make a state ballot in Pike and Monroe counties. In November 2019, she became the first Hispanic elected as school board director in the East Stroudsburg Area School District (ESASD), where she served a four-year term, chaired the Education Committee during her full tenure. She represented the ESASD on the Colonial Intermediate Unit 20 Board, where she was the first Hispanic and person of color appointed and served as vice president for three years out of her four-year term. Passionate about supporting professional organizations, she is a board member of the ACLU of Pennsylvania, Latina VIDA, Latinas on the Plaza and an advisory board member for several organizations including Monroe County Children and Youth, where she chairs the education committee and the League of Women Voters PA DEI steering committee.

Further accomplishments include serving as a gubernatorial appointee to Governor Tom Wolf's Latino Commission, where she served for six years and chaired the Statewide Education Committee, serving on the Brodhead Watershed Association Board, serving as vice president of Professional Development for Prospanica New York, serving on the Pennsylvania Department of Education Equity Task Force, where she chaired the Advocacy subcommittee and more efforts relating to social justice and equity at the local, state, and national levels.

Dr. Bonilla-Rodriguez was recognized as a 2014 Coors Light Lideres finalist and is the recipient of numerous awards, including a proclamation from the NYS Assembly, Proud to Be Latina Soy Poderosa award, Governor's Advisory Commission on Latino Affairs (GACLA) recognition award, SISGI Beyond Good Ideas Excellence in Nonprofit Leadership award, and Latino Diamante Comunidad. Her published written accomplishments include the books, *Gender, Race and Ethnicity in the Workplace and Today's Inspired Latina Volume II,* as well as contributing to the *Huffington Post* and being featured by several media outlets including, NBC Latino, Chief Writing Wolf, and the Empowered Latinas series.

While, she is proud of her many accomplishments, she highlights her greatest as being the mother of fourteen-year-old twin boys, Caleb and Joshua. She resides in Pennsylvania with her sons and husband, Robert. Her favorite quote is, "If I have seen further, it is by standing on the shoulders of giants." — Isaac Newton.

Twitter: Damary4lider
Instagram: drdamarybonillarodriguez
Facebook: DrDamary M. Bonilla-Rodriguez
LinkedIn: Damary Bonilla-Rodriguez, EdD
Website: drdamarybonillarodriguez.com

BIBLIOGRAPHY

- Anderton, Vix, "29 Quotes about Perfectionism to Change Your Perspective." LinkedIn.com. February 20, 2023. Accessed January 19, 2024. https://www.linkedin.com/pulse/29-quotes-perfectionism-change-your-perspective-vix-anderton-frsa.

- Anonymous. "30 Best Rigoberta Menchu Quotes with Image." Bookey.com. September 13, 2023. Accessed January 19, 2024. https://www.bookey.app/quote-author/rigoberta-menchu.

- Anonymous. "Factors Shaping an Identity: Internal & External." Study.com. Accessed January 19, 2024. https://study.com/academy/lesson/factors-influencing-identity-formation.html.

- APA Dictionary of Psychology. American Psychological Association. Accessed January 19, 2024. https://dictionary.apa.org/marianismo.

- Bonilla-Rodriguez, Damary M. "A Profile of Latina Leadership in the United States: Characteristics, Positive Influences, and Barriers." Rochester, NY, St. John Fischer University Fisher Digital Publications. Accessed January 19, 2024. https://fisherpub.sjf.edu/education_etd/38/.

- Bonilla-Rodriguez, Damary M. "Latinas and Modern Marianismo." *HuffPost.* December 25, 2013. Accessed January 19, 2024. https://www.huffpost.com/entry/latinas-and-modern-marianismo_b_4165200.

- Clance, Pauline Rose and Suzanne Imes. "The Imposter Phenomenon in High Achieving Women: Dynamics and Therapeutic Intervention." *Psychotherapy Theory, Research and Practice,* vol. 15, no. 3, Fall 1978. Accessed January 19, 2024. https://www.paulineroseclance.com/pdf/ip_high_achieving_women.pdf.

- Dorwart, Laura. "Understanding the Psychology Behind

Perfectionism." Verywell Health. September 19, 2023. Accessed January 19, 2024. https://www.verywellhealth.com/perfectionism-5323816#:~:text=Perfectionism%20is%20defined%20as%20the,%2C%20and%20unattainable%20goal%2Dsetting.

- Machismo in English. Cambridge Dictionary. Accessed January 19, 2024. https://dictionary.cambridge.org/us/dictionary/spanish-english/machismo.
- Swerdlow, Deborah. "Equal Pay Day: The Race and Gender Wage Gap." Idealist.com, Nov 1, 2023 10:00 a.m. Accessed January 19, 2024. https://www.idealist.org/en/careers/equal-pay-day-race-gender.
- Wasson, Donald L. "Second Triumvirate." World History Encyclopedia. April 18, 2016. Accessed January 19, 2024. https://www.worldhistory.org/Second_Triumvirate/.

Resources

1. https://www.betterup.com/blog/growth-mindset
2. https://youtube.com/watch?v=hiiEeMN7vbQ&si=1gpNxDCDTq6Qx0-M
3. https://www.amazon.com/s?k=7+habits+of+highly+effective+leaders&hvadid=580712368765&hvdev=t&hvlocphy=1018511&hvnetw=g&hvqmt=e&hvrand=17940428049573093404&hvtargid=kwd-2339980448&hydadcr=21937_13324267&tag=googhydr-20&ref=pd_sl_35foctkvqc_e
4. https://www.forbes.com/sites/womensmedia/2022/06/16/heres-how-your-personal-identity-and-sense-of-self-affect-your-growth/
5. https://youtube.com/watch?v=-tJKGZ_xSZ0&si=FFQJsBjNjcpUAmyb
6. https://www.amazon.com/Identity-Discover-Live-Life-Purpose/dp/0768408083/ref=asc_df_0768408083/?tag=hyprod-20&linkCode=df0&hvadid=312009828129&hvpos=&hvnetw=g&hvrand=2488127956642026922&hvpone=&hvptwo=&hvqmt=&hvdev=t&hvdvcmdl=&hvlocint=&hvlocphy=1018511&hvtargid=pla-453008384282&psc=1

7. https://neelraman.com/how-to-unlock-your-natural-gifts-to-achieve-your-big-dreams/
8. https://youtube.com/watch?v=qFLocdhL46I&si=RZKQWJgOnmwRQx1n
9. https://www.amazon.com/Discover-Your-Strengths-Marcus-Buckingham/dp/0743201140

www.ingramcontent.com/pod-product-compliance
Lightning Source LLC
Chambersburg PA
CBHW040800240426
43673CB00015B/401